SERMON OUTLINES
on

Spiritual Renewal

Charles R. Wood

PUBLICATIONS

Grand Rapids, MI 49501

Sermon Outlines on Spiritual Renewal

© 1969 by Charles R. Wood

Published by Kregel Publications, a division of Kregel, Inc.,
P.O. Box 2607, Grand Rapids, MI 49501. Kregel Publications
provides trusted, biblical publications for Christian growth and
service. Your comments and suggestions are valued.

For more information about Kregel Publications, visit our web
site at: www.kregel.com

Cover design: Frank Gutbrod

ISBN 0-8254-4126-9

1 2 3 4 5 / 04 03 02 01 00

Printed in the United States of America

Contents

Textual Index

Introduction

The messages selected for this book were all chosen on the basis of an initial premise — that revival is a very specific thing. We have often confused revival with various things such as the Christian life and evangelism, but revival is very specific. Revival is bringing back to life that which has lost its life. In the spiritual sense, it is renewal of the spiritual life in the individual who has grown cold and indifferent.

These sermon outlines are designed to challenge those who have grown cold and casual to a renewed interest in and appreciation of the Christian life. They are not primarily evangelistic in nature although they may be adapted to such purposes without too much effort. Recognizing that spiritual warmth and coldness are relative terms and concepts, the messages are designed to speak to an average congregation about the relative coldness and indifference which characterize many of God's people.

These sermons have been preached, and therefore, should be preachable. They have been used during a ten-year ministry in two different churches with great evidences of the blessing of God upon them.

Most of these messages are "expository" in nature. That is, they are designed to take a passage of Scripture, explain it, draw the main points from it and apply it to life. A study of the relevant passage prior to use of these outlines will be an absolute essential to their successful use.

The outlines which are marked "selected" or followed by the name of a source are borrowed from the works of others. The unmarked outlines are all the creation of the compiler of this series of outline books.

The prayer of the compiler is that God may use these messages to enhance the ministry of many of His servants and enrich the lives of many of His people.

Textual Index

What is Revival?

Introduction:

We hear a great deal about revival these days, but one has the feeling that many of those who talk much about it really know very little about it. Let's make an attempt to analyze just what is involved in revival:

I. What is Revival?
   A. Not evangelism even though many may be saved as a result of it.
   B. Not emotionalism although there may be emotional manifestations connected with it.
   C. It is a renewal of spiritual life in an individual or among a group of people.

II. When is Revival Needed?
   A. Whenever the love of God's people has waxed cold.
   B. What are the symptoms of its need?
      1. Spiritual complacency.
      2. Lack of concern for the lost.
      3. Harboring of secret sin.
      4. Animosity toward other Christians.
      5. An unforgiving spirit.
      6. Worldliness.
      7. Growth of pride.
      8. Any condition of spiritual standing in which we are in a state less than we formerly were.
   C. Dangers in our need for revival.
      1. Deteriorating change often comes without awareness (imperceptible).
      2. Often the condition of our hearts is such that we are not aware of our need at the very time it is greatest.
      3. The flesh tends to fight revival.

III. How Can We Have One?
   A. God is sovereign in its bestowal.
      1. Ultimately it comes when He wills it.
      2. There is no set pattern which will surely bring it.
      3. It is impossible to schedule a revival.
   B. There are certain conditions to meet to bring about the kind of situation into which God sends revival.
      1. Prayer — praying that God will send revival to His

people and to His work.
2. Facing of spiritual realities.
    a. Facing ourselves for what we are.
    b. Facing the nature of God.
    c. Facing the true nature of sin.
3. The confession of sin (to confess means to agree with God concerning sin).
4. Seeking of life on a higher plane than we have known it.

C. The problem of desire.
   1. Usually we don't want it badly enough to make any difference.
   2. God sometimes has to bring us to the end of ourselves before we desire to really know it.

Conclusion:

Revival is not turned off and on like a water fountain, but there are conditions which we must meet if a sovereign God is to bestow revival.

Recipe for Revival
I SAMUEL 7:1-17

Introduction:
Although God is sovereign in bestowal of revival in one sense, revival is always readily available in the life of the individual who meets certain conditions.

Israel was in trouble both spiritually and politically (with the Philistines). Samuel acted to help them with these two problems.

I. The Sickness Described (1 & 2)
A. The nature of Israel's illness.
   1. The ark is out of its proper place showing that God is out of the center of national life.
   2. There has been a rather long period of backsliding and estrangement.
B. The recognition of Israel's illness.
   1. The people lament for the Lord out of a sense of emptiness and a desire for restoration.
   2. The recognition arose as a result of oppression - this is a factor which God often uses to awaken.
C. Summary: People suffering from the spiritual sickness of being away from the Lord. The oppression of the Philistines and teaching of Samuel finally make them see their state.

II. The Treatment Prescribed (3)
A. Sincerity demanded.
   1. "Do you really want to return to the Lord?"
   2. If this is the desire of your hearts, certain things are necessary.
B. Steps of return suggested.
   1. Put away strange gods - refers to that which takes attention from the Lord.
   2. Center your hearts upon the Lord - this involves confession of sin.
   3. Serve the Lord - serve Him alone and not others.
C. Promises of return given - He will restore you to fellowship and will also deliver you.

III. The Remedy Applied (4-8)
A. The response of Israel.
   1. Immediately put away false gods and vow to serve the Lord.

      2.   Samuel gathers the people to a "revival meeting" at which the people:
         a.   Fast.
         b.   Confess their sin.
         c.   Sorrow over their sin.
  B. The reaction of the Philistines (7-9)
      1.   They hear of the meeting and decide to go against Israel.
      2.   The Israelites hear of their coming.
         a.   They are frightened.
         b.   They request prayer - they had learned to trust God through the experience of revival.
         c.   Samuel prays for them because convinced of their sincerity.

IV. The Healing Derived (10-14)

  A. Military victory is provided.
      1.   The battle (10 & 11). God thunders from heaven and the superstitious Philistines are routed.
      2.   The triumph (13 & 14). They regained peace and recaptured previously lost territories.
  B. A spiritual victory is provided (12).
      1.   People see God's power.
      2.   People are returned to fellowship.
      3.   Samuel takes steps to be sure it is remembered by setting up a marker and giving it a significant name.

Conclusion:

Israel starts out sick and oppressed and ends up with health and freedom. What happens in between is revival.

The Lord promises to restore those who have grown spiritually sick if they will face their problem and follow the steps He lays out for them.

Back to Bethel
GENESIS 31:13

Introduction:

Jacob had a variegated career. His character was checkered by deceit through much of his life. This is shown by his relationship to Bethel, the house of God. He had been to Bethel and had seen the Lord in a way that had changed his life. Time and distance had taken their toll, however, and there came a time when God ordered him back.

We have all had Bethel experiences in our lives and then seen them lost through the pressures of life and the passing of time. It may be that God would have us go back to Bethel.

I. What Was Bethel?

A. It was a geographical location near Luz where Jacob had passed a night of unusual blessing.

B. Beyond this, it was a place of great spiritual blessing.

C. It had also been a place of great victory.
1. God had spoken to Jacob.
2. Jacob had made a vow to God.
3. God had confirmed His promises to Jacob.

II. How did He Leave Bethel?

A. Jacob made two mistakes while there:
1. He centered on the place rather than on the Lord.
2. He made vows in the strength of the flesh.

B. Jacob then failed to cultivate the blessing.
1. Shown by his trickery with the cattle of Laban. Jacob saw to it that he got the best.
2. Entered into a time of "coming and going" rather than a time of the cultivation of the blessings of God.

C. Jacob then hit the downward skids:
1. It came following a great blessing (32:24-30).
2. The downward procession included:
    a. A failure to keep the faith (33:12-17).
    b. A tendency to lean on the world (33:18-20).
    c. Failure to reprove sin - tolerance for sin. It is ever the way that a downward path leads us to accept things we would formerly have flatly rejected.

III. How do We Get Back to Bethel?

A. Recognition: we must see where we are and recognize

11

how far we have drifted from the will of God.

B. Renovation: we need to deal with the problems in our lives both in confession and in forsaking.

C. Restoration: come back both to the place of blessing and the God of blessing.

Conclusion:

If we have gotten away from our Bethel, God is desirous that we return. We must recognize where we are, deal with the state in which we are and then renew our dedication as at our previous Bethel.

Achan and You

JOSHUA 7

Introduction:
We say that we are sick when only a part of us is sick, but this shows how part of something that is sick can make the whole entity ill. Sin in the life of one member in the body of believers can cause illness for the entire company.

This interesting story in the book of Joshua demonstrates how an entire group can be affected by the sin of one individual.

I. Its Historical Setting
    A. Follows crossing of Jordan river.
        1. The children of Israel had seen a marvelous demonstration of power.
        2. They were barely settled on the Canaan side.
    B. Follows the conquest of Jericho.
        1. This had been fully miraculous.
        2. This had contributed to their reputation both in the eyes of their enemies and their own eyes.

II. Its Narrated Story
    A. Improper preparations for conquest.
        1. Ai was the next natural city to conquer.
        2. Followed good military procedure.
        3. Underrated the enemy and took no time for recorded prayer.
    B. Humiliating defeat.
        1. Went in with great force and were defeated likely by smaller group.
        2. Both their egos and their reputations were damaged.
    C. Presumptuous prayer.
        1. Joshua tried to act as if the whole thing were God's fault.
        2. There is no evidence of humility in the reaction.
    D. Examining answer.
        1. God turned it back upon Joshua and blamed it on sin in the camp.
        2. God commanded an examination of sin, even giving details as to how it should be handled.

III. Its Important Implications
    A. Note the steps leading to failure.

1. Underrating the enemy.
2. Overestimation of personal strength.
3. Failure to seek the face of God.
B. Note the sin of Achan.
   1. Its nature: he took things wholly dedicated to God (saw, wanted, took).
   2. Its scope: the sin of one becomes the sin of all.
   3. Its treatment (as far as Israel was concerned): it had to be confessed and put away (in a very radical manner).
   4. Its terribleness: blessings were withheld by the Lord and a man had to die for the sin.

Conclusion:

We must be aware of sin in the camp and realize that the sin of one individual can become a bane to the entire company. Individual sin must be dealt with and put away before it begins to cost and then must be dealt with in a radical manner.

The Law of Requittal

JUDGES 1:7

Introduction:

Adoni-bezek had captured seventy kings and had treated them with harsh cruelty. In due time, he found himself the captive of another king and under the same kind of harsh treatment at his hand.

He, as many others since, found that with the measure one metes, it shall be measured to him again.

I. The Life of Man Cannot Escape Judgment

A. Man may deny it, but he cannot escape it.

B. Human affairs seem confused and tangled, but they are all part of a well-ordered plan to God.

II. Every Good Deed will be Honored with an Appropriate Reward

A. The law works both ways. "God is not unrighteous to forget your labor of love . . . "

B. Good deeds are to some degree their own reward.

C. Deeds done merely for the sake of reward are never good.

III. Though Justice be Long Delayed, It will come in Time

A. Adoni-bezek found this out.

B. God's hour is yet coming, and the man who feels that he has escaped is just being held in store for the day of wrath.

Conclusion:

The only hope for the future is in repentance for the past and the trust in the gospel of Jesus Christ to forgive sins and to make the heart over again.

-Selected

Contempt of God
I KINGS 14:9

Introduction:
When Jeroboam's child was sick, he sent his disguised wife to enquire of Ahijah the prophet of its final destiny. The Lord warned Ahijah of the coming of the queen and told him to tell her of the sick child's doom. The prophet also charged the king with having forsaken the Lord, having been ungrateful and having been an idolator.

I. **The Sin Charged Against Jeroboam**
  " . . . and hast cast me behind thy back . . . "
  A. This sin includes forgetfulness of God.
    1. Failure to remember God's goodness and mercy.
    2. Rejection of God as the grandest theme for the mind.
  B. This sin includes disregard for divine authority.
    1. Such defiance of God's authority is spiritual rebellion.
    2. The one who does not live in conformity to the commands of God lives in rebellion against God.
  C. This sin includes a determination on the part of the sinner to have his own way.

II. **The Consequences of this Sin**
  A. God will treat all such as He was treated by them.
  B. Such can expect no deliverance in the hour of sorrow and affliction.
    1. Demonstrated in the life of Jeroboam.
    2. If we shut out the light, we can expect the darkness.
  C. The eternal displeasure of God will rest upon all such in the world to come.

Conclusion:
The man who holds God in contempt will be held in contempt by God.

-Selected

Limping Along the Fence
I KINGS 18:21

Introduction:
God often presents us with great contrasts in the men He brings on the scene of history to live at the same time and to interact. Such is the case of Elijah, the dedicated prophet of God, and Ahab, the wicked, ruthless King of Israel.

Bring two men like this together, and someone is surely going to have a problem somewhere.

I. The Problem that Plagued the Prophet
To understand Elijah's problem, we must understand . . .
A. Ahab:
   1. Character - material strength coupled with spiritual weakness.
   2. Politics - the complete politician who decided everything on the basis of expediency (his marriage of Jezebel is thus explained).
   3. Religion - introduced Baalism to Israel.
B. Baalism:
   1. Came from Phoenicia along with Jezebel.
   2. Originally name for any god.
   3. Became the name for a god who was anything and everything which anyone could ever want (you name it; Baal was it).
C. Syncretism:
   1. Attempt to blend diverse elements into a one unity.
   2. Ahab attempted to blend worship of God and worship of Baal into a sort of superreligion.

The problem of the prophet was that Ahab had taught the children of Israel to worship both God and Baal.

II. The Choice that Challenged God's Children
"How long halt ye between two opinions? If the Lord be God, follow Him; but if Baal, then follow Him."
A. Elijah corrected the people's thinking by pointing out that they were actually faced with two choices rather than the one Ahab was trying to sell them.
B. Elijah described their conduct as "halting" which means to waver or totter.
C. Elijah reminded them of their responsibility by forcing them to come to a decision.

D. Elijah demanded action once the decision was made.
   1. Immediate action demanded - how long?
   2. Continuing action demanded - "follow Him" means go straight after.
E. Elijah demonstrated their folly by the contest on Carmel.

III. The Specifics that Scrutinize the Saints
Even though the story took place a long time ago, there are truths in it that speak to us today.
A. The church faces the same threat today as that posed by Ahab's syncretism.
   1. Materialism is a mixing of the God of the Bible and the god of this world.
   2. Most people today want to mix Christianity with other things.
B. The modern Christian faces options:
   1. It is just as deadly to waver today as it was then.
   2. He must be Lord of all or He is not Lord at all.
   3. The average Christian is stripped of power because he has not come to the place of really deciding for the Lord.

Conclusion:
When we begin to look for reasons for the failure of the modern church, we must give consideration to the fact that too many Christians are "limping along the fence."

The Tragedy of Missed Opportunity
EZRA 1:5-2:70

Introduction:
Life is a series of opportunities offered and choices faced. We are ever faced with decisions in every area of life, not the least of which is the spiritual. The Jews faced a choice in regard to an opportunity long ago, and the events of that incident are instructive for us now.

I. The Opportunity They were Offered
A. The decree of Cyrus - gave them the privilege of returning to their homeland in Palestine.
B. The backing of Cyrus.
   1. Gave them assurance of safety.
   2. Gave them a clear objective (rebuild the temple).
   3. Gave them back the captive temple vessels (1:7-11).
   4. Gave them other wealth to meet needs (1:6).
   5. Gave them necessary means of transportation.
   6. Even went so far as to force other people to help them.
C. The guarantee of success.
   1. Didn't mean that every single detail was perfectly worked out.
   2. Did mean that Cyrus had undertaken this as a personal project and thus had provided them with guaranteed success.
D. The challenging opportunity: an opportunity for a captive people who were deeply tied to their homeland to return to that homeland with the aid of a captor.

II. The Reaction to the Opportunity
A. The people rose up to return - chapter 2 records this.
   1. Obvious that only some of the exiles *chose* to return (note the number recorded in 2:64 and the word "some" in 2:70).
   2. Those who determined to return were hardly more than a small remnant.
B. Many people chose to remain in Babylon - truly strange in the light of the opportunity which faced them.
C. The reasons why they chose to remain there:

1. Some were comfortable there.
2. Some of them were too deeply involved with the life of Babylon to effectively break away.
3. Some were afraid it would cost them too much to leave.
4. Some were simply afraid of failure.
5. Some failed to recognize the enormity of the opportunity (history making events seldom look that way when the initial decisions are being made).

III. The Implications of the Story
A. The elements of human nature involved: we can draw the reasons why some refused to return from a knowledge of human nature: men missed then for the same reasons they miss now.
B. Opportunities are still missed:
1. Because we are too comfortable where we are to warrant taking the chances on missing and losing.
2. Because we are too much taken with the world.
3. Because the price looks as if it might be too high.
4. Because we are desperately afraid of failure.
5. Because we fail to realize the opportunity before us.
C. The application.
1. We are constantly faced with spiritual opportunities.
2. We tend to fail for the same reasons the Jews did.

Conclusion:

Let us squarely face the reasons why we hesitate and resolve to move beyond them. When God presents us with opportunities, let us not fail for the same reasons.

Wherewithal Shall a Young Man Cleanse His Way?

PSALM 119:9-11

Introduction:

In a day when it is difficult to find anyone who lives a clean life much less who really knows how, it is refreshing to find some very specific Biblical teaching regarding personal purity. It is possible, following the precepts laid down in the Word, to maintain purity of life even in a world known for its impurity.

I. A Pertinent Problem (verse 9a)
A. The statement: By what means can one who is younger maintain a life of purity and uprightness?
B. The meaning: How in the world am I going to keep my life clean in a world like this?

II. A Perfect Provision (verse 9b)
A. The answer provided:
1. The answer lies in the Word of God.
2. There are principles and precepts to answer every problem faced in modern life.
B. The answer validated:
1. What morality there is in society is based upon the Word of God.
2. Those who deny the Word of God usually want its precepts.
3. Even if Christianity were wrong, its precepts would still be worth having because they lead to a satisfied life.

III. A Probing Petition (verse 10)
A. "With my whole heart have I sought thee . . ."
1. This describes a heart totally dedicated to God and His will.
2. We often fail to find purity because we are not sufficiently convinced that it is really what we actually want.
B. "Let me not wander from thy commandments"
1. This expresses a desire for the life to be kept in conformity with the will of God.

2. Just the fact of praying this prayer shows the recognition on the part of the individual of the need for help (which help is available in the Lord).

IV. A Practical Presentation (verse 11)

    A. "Thy word have I hid in my heart . . ."
        1. Means to treasure, store up like a precious thing.
        2. Means far more than memorized - has to do with the total value we place upon the word of God.
    B. " . . . that I might not sin against God"
        1. A proper evaluation of the Word of God will be decisive in the battle with sin.
        2. The Word will keep us from sin; sin will keep us from the Word.

Conclusion:

It is possible to live a clean and decent life in this evil world. The Word of God provides the way in which this can be done. The challenge which comes to us is to determine whether or not we really want to live sin free.

The Bleating of Sheep
That Should Have Been Dead

I SAMUEL 15

Introduction:

God always has reason for what He does whether or not we can see it. God has been pictured as a "dirty bully" who enjoyed bloody Palestinian "Westerns."

This is just not so. Whenever He acted to exterminate people in the Old Testament, it was because they were so full of sin that action was necessary or because of treatment which they formerly had afforded His people.

The extermination called for here was for good reasons (cf. Exodus 17:8-16; Deuteronomy 25:17-19 and Numbers 24:20). The way it was carried out is very instructive for us.

I. The Command
  A. Its source was God.
  B. It was to destroy totally this people, their city and all their goods.

II. The Accomplishment
  A. It was carried out in part.
  B. Part was withheld (the bleating of the sheep revealed this).
  C. A lie was told to explain why the command was not fully carried out.
  D. God revealed the thing that was wrong.
    1. He showed the wrong of holding back.
    2. He showed that He would have been displeased even if these things had been held back for the reasons they claimed.

III. The Results
  A. The rejection of Saul. This was "the straw that broke the camel's back."
  B. The completion of the original command.

Conclusion:

The Lord requires complete obedience. Half measures even for the best causes are simply not enough for Him. Disobedience or partial obedience are worse than many of the sins which we consider major.

Solemn Pleadings for Revival
ISAIAH 41:1

I. **Let us be Silent**
    A. With solemn awe.
    B. With awe deepening to shame.
    C. With a silence of consideration.
    D. With a silence of attention.
    E. With submission.

II. **Let Us Renew Our Strength in that Silence.**
    A. By allowing time and space for the strengthening word to come into the soul and the energy of the Holy Spirit to be felt.
    B. By using this silence to consider who it is with whom we are dealing.
    C. By using this silence to meditate upon and remember His promises.
    D. By yielding up to God all our own wisdom and strength and casting ourselves upon the strength of God.

III. **Draw Near in Silence**
    A. Remember how near we really are.
    B. Remember we are coming to a Father.
    C. The desire to draw near is given by the Holy Spirit.
    D. The Lord loves to be pleaded with in prayer for His kingdom.

IV. **Let Us Speak Out of Silence**
    A. In adoring gratitude.
    B. In humble expostulation.
    C. In pleading.
    D. In confidence.

-Adapted from C. H. Spurgeon

A Glorious Glimpse of God
ISAIAH 6:1-4

Introduction:

While theologians are questioning the life and existence of God, the Bible speaks clearly of the living God. We can take a careful look at the living God through the experience and vision of Isaiah.

I. Its Setting
   A. The death of Uzziah.
      1. A good king who reigned 52 years (I Kings 15:1-7).
      2. Brought Israel into prosperity close to that of David.
      3. His death with much yet unaccomplished left frustration.
   B. Situation of Isaiah.
      1. In spite of chronology of book, he likely had not yet started his prophetic work.
      2. We know nothing of his early background, etc.
   C. The reality of the vision.
      1. Visions were fairly common in Old Testmant and had objective reality to those who saw them.
      2. What he saw corresponded with reality for him.

II. Its Descriptive Content
   There are six descriptions in the passage which tell us what he saw:
   A. God was on the throne, speaking of kingship and judgment - God is king and judge.
   B. The throne of God was high and lifted up, speaking of the exaltation of the heavenly king.
   C. His train filled the place - His kingly robe, showing the majesty of God, so filled everything that there was no room for anyone else.
   D. The seraphim cried, "Holy, Holy, Holy".
      1. They repeated it for emphasis (but at least hinted at the Trinity).
      2. It meant separateness essentially - separateness of God from evil and from creation (transcendence).
   E. The seraphim said, "The whole earth is full of His glory".
      1. This expresses a fact which can be observed by all

who have eyes properly focused to see.
2. God's glory consists of His revealed holiness and His revealed attributes.
F. The whole place was filled with smoke, which blurs the sight of God from sinful man and produces a solemn reverence and awe.

III. Its Effected Reactions
A. The seraphim.
1. Covered their faces in reverence and awe.
2. Covered their feet in a sign of humility and unworthiness.
3. Flew - proceeded to carry out the orders of the Lord.
4. Cried out in praise thus performing the greatest possible service, praising God.
B. The physical presence.
1. Post of the door moved in response to angelic praise.
2. The building itself could not remain unmoved in the presence of God.
C. The reaction of the man (Isaiah).
1. He was deeply moved.
2. He saw his sinfulness.
3. He showed a willing response.

Conclusion:

A doorpost proves wiser than men. It moves at the presence of God while men remain unmoved concerning His love and His will.

The Unpardonable Sin
MATTHEW 12:9-37

Introduction:

There has been much confusion concerning the nature of the unpardonable sin. Many sincere Christians have lived with a great deal of upset over the possibility of having been involved in something unpardonable.

Let's look at the facts in the passage and get an answer on this important question:

I. The Agitation (9-23)

A. An encounter over the Sabbath was the issue that triggered it.

B. Also involved some problems over healing:
   1. On the Sabbath (9-13).
   2. Of the multitudes (15).
   3. Of the demon possessed (21).

C. Stemmed from two sources:
   1. His rebuke of the Pharisees.
   2. The popular acclaim with which the people treated Him.

II. The Accusation (24)

They said He was casting out demons by the power of Satan.

A. Involved a tacit admission that He was casting out demons (there was admittedly something extraordinary to explain).

B. There was a designation of power - they said His power was from Beelzebub, the powerful prince of the demons.

III. The Answer (25-29)

A. Incongruous reasoning (25 & 26): something working against itself is in trouble. If Satan is casting out Satan, His kingdom shall fall.

B. Inconsistent reasoning (27): You claim the same power for your sons. Wouldn't the same charge apply to them as well?

C. Instructive reasoning (28 & 29): Having been driven to a conclusion, you should be willing to accept something - that casting out demons involves a restraint on the king of demons, Satan.

IV. **The Application (31-37)**
   A. Condemnation of human tendency to obscure issues (30).
      1. They were trying to cloud over the simple.
      2. He simply says, "It has to be this or that".
   B. Condemnation of human blasphemy (31 & 32).
      1. The unpardonable sin:
         a. It must be tied to its context.
         b. Its definition: attributing to Satan the work of God's Spirit.
         c. It is unpardonable partly because a man is already beyond hope when he gets to this point in life.
      2. Cautions on the unpardonable sin:
         a. This is a sin against light.
         b. It is a deliberate sin.
         c. No Christian need fear it.
   C. Condemnation of human inconsistency (33-37).
      1. Bring your practice into line with reality.
      2. The words reveal the man (this is why words are made the basis of condemnation here).
      3. Even the idle word is important because of what it reveals of man.

Conclusion:

The person outside Christ stands in danger of the unpardonable sin. The person in Christ ought to order his life so that he never lives in a way which would agree with the problems of the Pharisees.

God's Knowledge of Sin

AMOS 5:1 & 2

Introduction:

We try to kid ourselves into thinking that God is not conscious of our sin. The truth of the matter is that He is much more conscious of our sin than we ourselves.

I. This Knowledge Asserted

Impenitent men are so under the binding influence of sin that they imagine God is unacquainted with them.

A. Actually God sees them in all their extent and variety.
1. From infancy to age.
2. Both of omission and commission.
3. Of word, thought and deed.

B. God also sees them in all their heinousness.
1. He sees them as being against light and knowledge.
2. He sees them as being against vows and resolutions.
3. He sees them as being against God's merciful judgments.

II. The Effect this Divine Knowledge Should Have

A. It should produce sorrow for sin.
B. It should induce confession of sin.
C. It should create in us a determination to forsake sin.
D. It should call forth a prayer to God for the forgiveness of sin.

Conclusion:

Our sins are not hidden from God. They are seen by Him, and we do well to realize that fact and deal with them before He begins to so do.

-Selected

Denial, Crucifixion and Discipleship
MATTHEW 16:21-28

Introduction:

There were a number of "turning points" in the ministry of Christ. Such a "turning point" is before us in the passage: "From that time forth began Jesus . . ." He will now begin to concentrate on teaching about the crucifixion.

At the same time His teaching takes a new direction, the disciples enter into a new period — one of misunderstanding.

I. **The Conflict that Clarified the Issue**
   A. Christ's declaration (verse 21) introduced something new.
      1. The word "must" modified each clause in the verse (e.g., He must go up to Jerusalem, He must be crucified, etc.).
      2. This is a clear statement of what was yet to come.
   B. Peter's remonstrance (22)
      1. Peter took Him aside and began to rebuke Him, using strong language (e.g., "God forbid").
      2. Peter's problem was that:
         a. He couldn't reconcile this teaching with what Christ had said on previous occasions.
         b. He felt that he must continue to be the spokesman.
   C. Christ's rebuke (23)
      1. He cut Peter off (Peter was not Satan but had allowed his lips to be used of Satan thus playing the role of Satan to Christ at this point).
         a. Peter failed to see "the things of God" - eternal purposes (the "musts" mentioned earlier).
         b. Peter had his mind on "the things of men."
      2. Points out a danger:
         a. The possibility of becomming (even if only temporarily) Satan's tool or man.
         b. The possibility of misunderstanding the purposes of God.
         c. The possibility of placing human will before God's.

II. **The Correction that Chartered the Course (24)**
   A. An initial condition.

1. "If any man will come after me . . ."
2. Stresses the fact that there are always options in discipleship.
B. The detailed demands:
   1. " . . . let him deny himself . . . " - renounce himself as the center of concern and attention.
   2. " . . . let him take up his cross (daily) . . . " - cheerfully bear the suffering, shame and loss directly connected with the following of Christ.
   3. " . . . let him follow me . . . " - pattern his life on mine (in contrast to what Peter has just done).
C. The present implications.
   1. We are also faced with a discipleship option.
   2. The same three elements are involved for us.
   3. We are too much "minded with the things of men."

III. The Reasons that Ramify the Requirements

A. Reason I: "For whosoever will save his life shall lose it . . ."
   1. The one who sets up the physical and temporal as ultimate will ultimately lose; the one who counts the physical as little will win the real life.
   2. Stated: Be a disciple, for the physical life is not the real life.
B. Reason II: "For what is a man profited if he shall gain the whole world and lose his own soul . . ."
   1. What's the use of winning the world and losing the soul? What can a man swap for his soul?
   2. Stated: Be a disciple because of the overwhelming importance of the soul and its destiny.
C. Reason III: "For the Son of Man shall come in the glory of His Father . . ."
   1. Predicts the second coming which will not only be glory but also power.
   2. Stated: Be a disciple He is going to come and reward the way in which we live.

Conclusion:

Christ starts to teach about the nature of His kingdom. Peter interrupts and intrudes the things of men into the discussion. Christ then delineates the demands and presents reasons why we should follow after Him.

Three Tents on the Mountain
MATTHEW 17:1-13

Introduction:
  If it is human to say a dumb thing at a crucial time, and it is, then Peter was indeed human. Here is Peter on a mountaintop in the presence of the divine and the eternal, and he says, "Let us make three huts."

I. Peter Failed by Failing to Hear what Christ was Trying to Tell Him
  A. The transfiguration was for the disciples: Christ did not need this, but they did, and that is why they were witnesses.
  B. It was designed to show.
    1. The truthfulness of some previous statements:
      a. Peter's confession of faith (16:16).
      b. Christ's declaration of impending death (16:21).
    2. The glorious nature of Christ.
    3. The superiority of Christ to all others - Moses and Elijah were there as representatives of Law and Prophets. They disappeared, and the disciples saw no one save Jesus only.
    4. The approval of God on all Christ's words and deeds: Note the voice —
      a. Identification - this is my beloved Son.
      b. Satisfaction - in Whom I am well pleased.
      c. Injunction - Hear ye Him.
  C. Peter missed the whole point.
    1. Christ was teaching that they must go on to Jerusalem where He would die in the plan of God. Peter was saying, "Let us stay here."
    2. God was teaching that Christ was superior to all. Peter tried to make Him one of equals by building three huts.
    3. We often fail for the same reason Peter did - we aren't quiet long enough to hear what God is trying to say to us.

II. Peter Failed by Failing to Understand the Nature of Spiritual Lessons
  A. The whole event was spiritual in nature - an otherworldly radiance, otherworldly visitors and an other-

worldly voice.
- B. The whole event was designed to reach spiritual truth.
  1. The nature of death - Peter, James and John were here. They were with Him three times when He taught about death:
     a. House of Jairus - Christ's power over death.
     b. Transfiguration - Christ's triumph over death.
     c. Garden of Gethsemane - Christ's yieldedness to death.
  2. That the path to glory lay through suffering.
- C. Peter missed the point again.
  1. He was too busy building thatched huts in his mind.
  2. We get so busy building tabernacles (good works, church attendance, conformity, reputation, etc.,) that we miss spiritual truths also.

III. Peter Failed by Trying to Step Ahead of God
- A. God was making His purposes clear - He was confirming Christ's statement and giving more details (Luke 9:30 & 31).
- B. Peter sought to intervene.
  1. He said, "Let's stay here."
  2. Actually saying, "Here, yes; there, no!" and "Glory, yes; suffering, no!"
- C. Peter gave a remarkable demonstration of humanity.
  1. He set his will over against God's.
  2. We tend to do this same thing in the areas that Peter invaded - suffering and where the details are not clear.

IV. Peter Failed by Trying to Contain God in Temporal Quarters
- A. They were in the presence of eternity - the glory and the visitors both showed this.
- B. Peter sought to confine the whole thing in time.
  1. Booths are thatched roofed huts.
  2. In wanting to construct such huts, Peter made several mistakes:
     a. That Christ *could be* thus contained.
     b. That Christ and His visitors *would be* thus contained.
     c. That Christ and His visitors *needed to be* thus contained.

C. He thus revealed much of our own problem.
    1. We also try to get God into temporal quarters such as a building, our human conceptions or our finite minds.
    2. We usually end up with inadequate conceptions of God and a God that is truly too small.

V. Peter Failed by Trying to Hold Today's Blessings for the Future
  A. There was much yet to come in the plan of God.
    1. More teaching.
    2. A sojourn in the valley (14-21).
    3. Some lessons to be learned about power, responsibility and Christ.
  B. Peter would have settled to hold on there on the mountain.
  C. Christ made plain other purposes.
    1. Led them down the mountain.
    2. Told them to tell no one.
      a. Because the next theme was the cross not the glory.
      b. Because they needed to wait for the H.S. to help them tell it.
      c. Because visions are of little value except to those who see them.
      d. Because this would have tended to make them live on it.
  D. Clear message here for us.
    1. The valley often follows the mountains.
    2. We must enjoy today's blessings today.
    3. Our experience needs to be new each day - can't live on yesterday's.

Conclusion:
Peter spoke at a crucial time and revealed enormous failure
-to hear what Christ was trying to tell him
-to understand spiritual lessons
-by trying to step ahead of God
-by trying to cram the divine into a little temporal box
-by trying to make today's blessings last until tomorrow.
But Peter's main failure was one of self-will. We fail in the same ways for the same reason.
We are told that Peter learned (II Peter 1:15-18). The big question is, "Will we learn?"

Choosing the Better Part
LUKE 10:38-42

Introduction:

Life involves a continuing sequence of choices which all of us must face. One of the most difficult things in this whole matter of choices is making wise ones. Two sisters had to make a choice in this passage. What they chose and what Christ had to say about it is very instructive.

I. A Study in Contrasts
   A. Mary - the younger sister:
      1. "Sat at the feet of Jesus" - had come to absorb teaching.
      2. "Heard His word" - she was listening intently to the exclusion of everything else.
   B. Martha - the older sister:
      1. She received Christ into her house - demonstrated discipleship by the extension of hospitality.
      2. She was busily involved in service - was serving the Lord by trying to make His stay more pleasant.
      3. She suffered, however, from a bad attitude - she had grown weary in service, became resentful of her sister's failure to help and was letting her attitude show.

II. A Rebuke of Contention
   Christ answered Martha's cross challenge:
   A. He spoke to her in tenderness "Martha, Martha" - repetition shows the tenderness of His word to her.
   B. He analyzed her attitude:
      1. He saw her as "careful" or filled with care within.
      2. He saw her as "troubled" or hurried and rushed as a result of her inner state of care.
      3. He saw her as "fixed on many things" or occupied and distracted about an host of things.
   C. He defined her problem:
      1. Many things had crowded out the "one thing needful" - service is only wrong when it becomes a substitute, which it had for her.
      2. The "one thing needful" was time and thought devoted to Him, a quiet time with attention fixed on Him.

III. An Evaluation of Choice
A. Christ makes a declaration:
   1. Mary had made the better choice (she had chosen service with devotion rather than service without devotion).
   2. Her choice was not to be taken away from her (He actually refused to act on Martha's request).
B. The reason for the evaluation:
   1. Mary had chosen: communion, instruction, worship, growth and preparation.
   2. If Martha had done so, she would not have been so fretted up and could have served better.
C. The lessons of the evaluation:
   1. Sometimes we have to chose between devotion with service or service without devotion.
   2. We need to learn what Martha needed to learn:
      -effective service is dependent upon effective devotion.
      -lack of devotion results in frustration and tension.

Conclusion:
Having chosen to sit at the feet of Jesus, Mary was complemented on having made a wise choice. Martha was rebuked, not for her service, but for her attitude in service which came as a result of her devotional failure.

Distant Following

Introduction:

Peter presents a strange mixture of strength and weakness, courage and cowardice.

Sometimes he shows himself in a manner that calls for our admiration, and at other times he acts in such a way as to cause us to look upon him with wonder and pity. But let us not forget that we may resemble Peter in following Christ afar off. Alas! many do.

Consider the *causes* and *perils* of following Christ at a distance.

I. The Causes of Following Afar Off

In Peter's case various causes were at work, but they were all in himself. So far as Christ was concerned, there was no reason why Peter should not have followed closely.

A. *One cause of Peter's following was the fear of man.*
  1. "The fear of man brought a snare." It made Peter a coward.
  2. Many are like Peter in this respect. They are afraid to be too closely identified with Christ and His cause lest they should suffer persecution.
B. *Want of love might in part account for Peter's conduct.*
  1. He did love Christ even then, but not sufficiently to keep *near* Him. A stronger love would have made him a braver man.
  2. Weakness of love is often a cause of distant following.
C. *Possibly weakness of faith was another cause.*
  1. Christ had prayed that Peter's faith might not fail, and it did not fail, but it might become *weak.*
  2. After the arrest of Jesus, doubts *might* arise in Peter's mind.
D. *Worldliness is often a cause of distant following.* "No man can serve two masters," but some Christians do seem to try to serve Christ and the world, with the result that Christ is served but *indifferently.*
E. *A misconception of what Christ requires is another cause of distant following.*
  Faith is not all that Christ requires, yet some seem to think it is.

He requires warm attachment, zealous service, self-denial, and open acknowledgment.

II. The Perils of Following Afar Off
    A. *In Peter's case following afar off was the beginning of a dreadful fall.*
        1. He followed at a distance, and then fell into the heinous sin of denying Christ.
        2. Distant following is often succeeded by a fall.
        3. Backsliding is in most cases due to following afar off.
    B. *Another evil consequence of distant following is the loss of inward peace and joy.*
        1. Though a Christian may follow Christ at a distance without falling into *open sin*, he cannot do so without loss of spiritual good.
        2. The profession of religion may be retained when the *joy* of it is lost.
        3. Again, loss of usefulness is a result of following afar off. A Christian's usefulness depends on the vitality, thoroughness, and consistency of his religious life.

Conclusion:

Let those who are conscious of following Christ afar off be encouraged to come near to Him. "Lay aside every weight." Seek the Spirit's help. Watch and pray.

-G. Charlesworth

Factions and Foolishness
I CORINTHIANS 1:1-31

Introduction:
The Corinthian church, of all the New Testament churches, was one which faced enormous problems as it sought to do the will of God. Paul writes both the Corinthian epistles in an effort to combat some of the problems which plagued that church.

I. The Position of the Church (1-9)
    A. Its address: (1-3).
        1. A "church of God."
        2. Composed of saints.
        3. Made up of those *"called* to be saints."
    B. Its endowment (4-9).
        1. The grace of God (4).
        2. Spiritual enrichment (5).
        3. Confirmed testimony (6).
        4. Second to none in many things (7a).
        5. Expectant of the Lord's return (7b).
        6. Sure in the day of judgment (8).
        7. Fellowshipping with a faithful God (9).

II. The Problem of the Church (10-31)
The basic problem was that they were not living according to their position.
    A. A division described (10-12).
        1. The key "divisions among you" (10).
            a. Report of this had come to Paul (11).
            b. It is inevitable that divisions and contentions go together.
        2. The situation.
            a. Four parties present (including the "Christ" party).
            b. All four, including the "Christ" party, were wrong.
    B. The division explored and exploded (13-17).
        1. Three searching questions asked (13).
            a. Is Christ divided?
            b. Was Paul crucified for you?
            c. Were you baptized in the name of Paul?
        2. The argument exploded (14-17).
    C. Solutions suggested (18-31).

1. Two real problems involved.
   a. Adherence to human wisdom.
   b. Personal pride.
2. Two real problems attacked.
   a. The uselessness of human wisdom shown (18-25).
   b. The bubble of pride burst (26-31).

Conclusion:

This is a letter designed for all churches. It declares that a divided church is the result of carnality which shows itself in desire for human wisdom and personal pride of position.

The solution to carnality-caused divisions lies in recognizing the superiority of God's wisdom and recognizing the insignificance of self.

Review, Rewards and Regrets
I CORINTHIANS 3:1-23

Introduction:

I Corinthians was written to a church with problems so it is not surprising that it deals a great deal with problems. One of the greatest problems in the Christian world is dealt with in the passage before us - carnality.

I. The Nature of Carnality
    A. Paul has shown two contrasting things previously.
        1. The spiritual - the saved man.
        2. The natural - the unsaved man.
    B. He now introduces a new contrast.
        1. The spiritual man - full grown and spiritually mature.
        2. The carnal man - immature, ungrown (baby in Christ), unable to bear the really deep things of God.

II. The Character of Carnality.
    A. It shows itself in divisions and splits (verses 3 & 4).
    B. It shows itself in temporal interests having priority (verse 12).
    C. It shows itself in moral defilement (verses 16 & 17).
    D. It shows itself in affection for human wisdom (verses 18-20).
    E. It shows itself by glorying in men rather than in God (verse 21).

III. The Folly of Carnality
    A. It prevents growth (verses 1 & 2) - one can't grow in grace through feeding on the world.
    B. It violates principles of good reasoning (verses 5-8) - logic shows that the fruit of carnality (division) is always foolish.
    C. It misunderstands God's purposes (verses 9-11) - God's purposes run just completely counter to carnality.

IV. The Cure of Carnality
    A. Realization of coming judgment (verses 12-15).
        1. All our spiritual building will be judged.
        2. There will be loss for failure to produce.
    B. Recognition of certain facts (verse 16 & 17, 22 & 23).

     1. You are the Temple of the Holy Ghost.
     2. God desires to dwell in you and do His work in you.
     3. He has provided everything needed for spiritual living.
  C. Reappraisal of self (verses 18-20).
     1. We must view ourselves as God does.
     2. We must yield and confess wherein God shows us we are wrong.

Conclusion:

Most problems in the modern church stem from carnality. Are you one of the carnal people who causes so many problems and hinder the work of the Lord?

The Old Man is Dead
II CORINTHIANS 5:17

Introduction:
So often our practice isn't in accord with our beliefs, and this affects all of life. We speak of "the new man in Christ Jesus" but live just like the old man used to live. A review of the Bible's teaching about the old man may be of help in bringing our living in line with our believing.

I. **A Statement of Fact**
   A. An action viewed as accomplished - old things are already passed away.
   B. An action explained - what are the old things that have passed away?
      1. Not in physical or material sense (arthritis, a leaky roof, etc.).
      2. Obviously the spiritual which is spoken of here. Includes: sinful habits, lusts, patterns of life, spiritually related personality problems, internal spiritual disorders (pride, hate, stubbornness), etc.
   C. An action reversed - all things are become new (this is also viewed as having already taken place).
   D. An excitement engendered - "Behold" is an attention-getter.

II. **An Argument from Experience**
   A. This is contrary to much common experience in which one is saved, freed from old habits and then doomed to the return of many of the habits.
   B. We tend to live the opposite way - old things are not only alive but actually dominant keeping us from showing our Christianity.
   C. This raises serious questions - are the Scriptures wrong or should they be somehow retranslated?
   D. Why are the Scriptures and experience so often so far apart?

III. **A Scriptural Answer**
   A. God has made a provision; sin was covered on Calvary. As far as God is concerned, sin is cared for. The answer must lie elsewhere.
   B. We are the problem; we fail to appropriate what God has done for us. Actually we, rather than the Scriptures, need the new translation.

C. God has even provided the answer to this problem (Galatians 5:16; Ephesians 4:17-24; Philippians 2:5-11; Colossians 3:5-15).

Conclusion:

God has accomplished certain things for us, things which can set us free. The question rests with what we are willing to do with what He has accomplished.

The Expectations of God
ROMANS 12:1

Introduction:
The most common cause of failure in the business world is lack of understanding of the nature of one's responsibilities. This is often due to the inability or failure of a supervisor to make clear what is expected of a worker.

How wonderful that God never fails to let us know what He expects of us as we live the Christian life.

I. God's Specific Request
"I beseech you . . . brethren . . . that ye present your bodies a living sacrifice . . . "
- A. The meaning:
    1. The body must be surrendered because only in that way can it be demonstrated that the will has been surrendered.
    2. A sacrifice is something given to God as an expression of homage or thanksgiving.
- B. The manner:
    1. This is put in the form of a request - "I beseech you."
    2. Surrendered living is always an optional matter (we may pay a price if we make the wrong decision, but we are given the opportunity of making the decision none-the-less).

II. God's Additional Requirements
There are certain qualifications which go with this request.
- A. "Brethren" - This is an appeal pointed to the saved alone.
- B. "Living" - God wants us to be living in a living Christianity.
- C. "Holy" - word originally meant "whole" and later came to mean "pure". Both meanings are valid:
    1. We are to give Him the totality of our lives.
    2. We are to give Him the purity of our lives.
- D. "Acceptable unto God" - means "well-pleasing, giving of satisfaction."

III. God's Particular Reasons
Sometimes we make a request of someone without giving reasons for what we desire; God seldom does it that way.

A. " . . . therefore, by the mercies of God . . . "
   1. "Therefore" looks back to what has come before in the book.
   2. We can trace the mercies of God chapter by chapter in Romans and discover a perfectly good reason for God's request.
B. " . . . which is your reasonable service."
   1. Means something which has been carefully reasoned through.
   2. We should surrender to Him because that is what good reasoning tells us we should do.

Conclusion:

Here is what God expects of us: request, requirement, reason.

What you do with it is up to you!

Grieve Not the Holy Spirit
EPHESIANS 4:25-32

Introduction:

If we really accept the Biblical teaching concerning the personality of the Holy Spirit of God, we will not have any great trouble attributing the characteristics of personality to Him. The Bible teaches that He is a person and that He is subject to many of the same feelings and emotions common to personality.

The passage before has some very solemn things to say about our treatment of the personality of the Holy Spirit.

I. An Unpleasant Possibility

"Grieve not the Holy Spirit of God . . . "

A. The Spirit of God can be grieved. He can easily be made sorrowful concerning specific things.

B. How is the Holy Spirit grieved? There are several indications in the passage:
1. Lying (verse 25).
2. Anger (verse 26).
3. Yielding to temptation (verse 27).
4. Stealing (verse 28).
5. Corrupt communications (verse 29).
6. Disordered interpersonal relationships (verses 31 & 32).

II. A Particular Aspect

Let us look at the last of the above list — disordered interpersonal relationships:

A. The presence of certain things is grieving, and thus these things should be put off:
1. Bitterness - bitter hatred.
2. Wrath - sudden outbursts of boiling anger.
3. Anger - gradual buildup of hatred and resentment with eye to vengeance.
4. Clamor - the noise made by people who are shouting back and forth in a quarrel.
5. Evil speaking — slanderous, injurious speech about someone's character.
6. All malice - a vicious disposition.

B. The absence of certain things is grieving, and thus these things should be put on:
1. Two qualities of character.

        a. "Be ye kind to one another" - mild, pleasant, kind, beneficial.

        b. "Tenderhearted" - compassionate.

    2. An underlying principle - "forgiving one another."

        a. Most failure to have right relationships is failure to forgive.

        b. This is to be done "even as God for Christ sake hath forgiven you."

III. A Serious Result

A. An adverse relationship between the Spirit and the Christian.

B. The Spirit must turn from a ministry *through* us to a ministry *to* us.

C. Note that the Spirit's ministry is limited in us, but He does not depart from us.

IV. A Suggested Solution

A. Answer suggested by the text: put off and put on.

B. Comes as we allow the Holy Spirit to work in our hearts and lives.

Conclusion:

It is a serious business to grieve the Holy Spirit. It is most important to make it right any time we feel that we may have done so. Right relationship with the Holy Spirit is essential to all other right relationships in life.

Why We Preach
I TIMOTHY 1:5

Introduction:

Preaching could be a very discouraging business, but the interposition of the power of the Lord keeps it from becoming that. Actually we are preaching in service to God and to effect changes in the lives of men.

In writing to young Pastor Timothy, Paul discusses this. He says that the real purpose of the Word is LOVE:

I. From A Pure Heart
A. Speaks of the center of the emotional life and the will.
B. The most important part of man.
   1. Out of it are the issues of life.
   2. A man is actually what he thinks in his heart.
C. Its purity is most important.
   1. Without a pure heart, man can't see God (Matthew 5:4).
   2. Without a pure heart, man is wretched (Psalm 32: 3 & 4; 51:10).
   3. The presence of sin is what keeps it from purity.
   4. Only way to a pure heart is through the blood of Christ.

II. From A Good Conscience
A. This is the inner voice which passes judgment on our actions as to whether or not we really approve of what we are doing.
B. The conscience is trainable.
   1. Can be seared by constant misuse and brought to the place where it is no longer valid.
   2. Can be trained to become a useful tool for right.
C. We are born with a good conscience - what we do with it afterward is somewhat up to us.
D. The conscience has tremendous importance for us because no one can judge us quite as accurately as we can judge ourselves.
E. The pathway to a good conscience is also through Christ — it is the Word of God that instructs the conscience properly.

III. From an Unfeigned Faith
A. A faith that is sincere — whether it be our Christian

49

beliefs or our actual faith in Christ.
B. Of tremendous importance.
   1. Presence of so much spurious faith is the reason many turn away.
   2. One of the easiest things there is to counterfeit (up to a certain point).
   3. Only a genuine faith can get you to God.
C. Is yours sincere?
   1. What are you trusting in?
   2. How are you trusting?
   3. Is this the commitment of the whole of your life?

Conclusion:
We preach to produce love from a pure heart, from a good conscience and from a sincere faith. Do you have these three ingredients in your life?Only God can actually give them to you by His Holy Spirit.

Hardening of the Arteries
HEBREWS 3:7-13

Introduction:

There is an interesting passage here in Hebrews that quotes at length a passage from the Old Testament in an effort to help us learn from the experience of the Old Testament saints. Our situations are often so parallel that it is well to explore the situation.

I. The Sin that Brought the Warning
   A. Quotes Psalm 95 that refers to experience of Israel in the wilderness.
   B. The specific situation:
      1. Israel guilty of continued sin:
         a. Demand for bread (Sin).
         b. Demand for water (Meribah).
         c. The golden calf (Sinai).
         d. The demand for meat (Taberah).
      2. Culmination of sin comes at Kadesh (Numbers 14:22 & 23; 28-30).
         a. Spies return with majority and minority reports.
         b. The majority report is accepted even though the minority report speaks the will of God.
         c. The people reject the hand of God, and He dooms them to wandering.
   C. The particular sin:
      1. Involves many items: murmuring, dissatisfaction, disobedience, apostasy.
      2. The basic issue: failure to hear and heed the Lord.

II. The Warning that Reproved the Sin
   A. Expressed desire - "Oh, that ye would hear . . . ". God always desires a listener.
   B. Expressed fear - that they would harden their hearts and thus become insensible to the leading of the Lord.
   C. Expressed likeness - compares the readers with their forefathers who would not hear or heed the Lord.
   D. Expressed condemnation - God was grieved with them because of their hardened hearts.
   E. Expressed consequences - the price they paid for failure was failure to "enter into rest" in the promised land.

III. The Implications that Address Our Situation
A. The issues at stake:
  1. An evil heart of unbelief.
  2. A hardening through the deceitfulness of sin.
  3. A provoking of God.
B. The dangers we face:
  1. Missing the blessing of God.
  2. Missing the correction of God.
  3. Missing God completely.
C. The way it works:
  1. God speaks: in the Word, preaching, conscience, circumstances and the admonitions of others.
  2. Each time we refuse to hear and heed, the hardening increases.
  3. There can come a time when God stops speaking and starts acting.
D. The application:
  1. Is God speaking to you about something in your life?
  2. Are you refusing to listen?
E. The cure:
  1. Exhort one another.
  2. Take heed to the speaking voice of God.

Conclusion:

God forbid that we should suffer the same fate as Israel for the same reasons.

The Publican in the Temple
LUKE 18:13 & 14

Introduction:
This is a well-known story of religious reactions on the part of two men. The reaction of the publican is especially instructive for us.

I. Note the Admission of Personal Guilt
    A. "God be merciful to me a sinner". He recognized his state.
    B. He also stressed the fact that he himself was the sinner. There is ever a need for us to separate ourselves from the crowd and face God as individuals.

II. Note the Passionate Grief
He showed great distress because of sin. This was produced by:
    A. Realization of the deep offenses he had offered God. "Against thee, and thee only have I sinned."
    B. Realization of the awful injury we have afflicted upon ourselves. In sinning against God, we sin against our own souls.
    C. Realization of the evil influence he had asserted on others.

III. Note the Deep Humility Mingled with Shame
    A. Shown by standing afar off. He felt unworthy to get closer.
    B. Shown by the fact that he would not even lift up his eyes to heaven.

IV. Note the Earnest Prayer to Heaven
    A. The object of this prayer is mercy.
    B. The character of the prayer:
        1. Is simple and brief.
        2. Is sincere and earnest.
        3. It is presented at the time of God's appointment (note that he went up to the temple to pray).

Conclusion:
This man went down to his house justified.

-Selected

Things That Hinder Spiritual Growth
HEBREWS 5:12-14; I PETER 3:18

I. Growth is Hindered by Neglecting God's Word (I Peter 2:2).
The Bible is the book of necessary instruction for the believer. (Psalms 119:9; 73:24 and Isaiah 8:20)

II. Growth is Hindered by Following False Teachers (II Peter 3:16-18).
If you turn aside from the teaching of the Word, spiritual growth ceases. (II Timothy 3:1-7; 4:7; II Peter 2:1 & 2).

III. Growth is Hindered by Failing to Control the Tongue (James 3:2).
The misuse of the tongue can defeat all the spiritual advances which we make. (James 3:16 & 17; Titus 2:8; I Timothy 6:1-5).

IV. Growth is Hindered by Showing Partiality Among Brethren (James 2:1-4).
This can cultivate a spirit between ourselves and others that will result in hindered growth. (James 3: I Timothy 5:20 & 21; Romans 12:10).

V. Growth is Hindered by Making Excuses (Exodus 3:11; 4:1).
We usually excuse ourselves from doing the very things that will make us strong. (Philippians 4: 13, 19; John 15:5; Luke 14:18, 24).

VI. Growth is Hindered when We Neglect the Means of Grace Provided for Us (Hebrews 10:15).
Prayer, worship, fellowship, the Lord's table and God's word are all designed to help us grow. If we neglect them, we won't grow. (Acts 2:42; Titus 2:12; I Corinthians 11:30).

VII. Growth is Hindered by Alliances with the World (Hebrews 13:13).
This is illustrated by what it cost Jehoshaphat to help Ahab. (II Corinthians 6:14-18; I John 2:15-17; Matthew 6:19-24).

-C.C. Maple

Resist the Devil
JAMES 4:7

Introduction:
Believers are called upon not only to contend with an evil heart and an evil world, but also with evil spirits. "We wrestle . . . against the rulers of the darkness." These adversaries are banded together under one head. In speaking of the devil, we must include all his emissaries.

I. The Foe
It is a mistake to underrate the importance of an enemy. Therefore let us form a right estimate of our foe:
A. His power: he can inflame the mind and the evil desires of the soul. His power is enormous but is limited by the totality of power in our God.
B. His diligence: he is represented as continually "going about seeking whom he may devour." If repulsed a hundred times, he only tries again.
C. His malice: he envies every human happiness and seeks to undermine it.
D. His policy: he is crafty and subtle. He is a hidden assassin rather than an open foe.
E. His experience: he has long studied human nature so he is very adept at deceiving mankind.

II. The Fight
We are called upon to resist rather than to fight the devil. We are not to parley or dialogue with him, but rather to resist him at every turn.
A. General orders:
1. Be sober both physically and mentally.
2. Be vigilant.
3. Be united - stand shoulder to shoulder with your allies.
B. Tried weapons:
1. The Word of God.
2. Past experience. When Satan tries to tell you how little God will do for you, cry aloud what God has done for you.
3. Earnest prayer. Allow God to become engaged in the conflict with you.
C. Impenetrable (Ephesians 6:10-18).

III. The Flight
The word says, "he will flee from you." It may not be at first for there must be real resistance to his power.
- A. In this life, the flight is temporary. He leaves only to return. Each engagement, however, equips us the more to stand fast the next time.
- B. In the future, there will be final flight. He shall flee never to return again (Romans 16:20).

Conclusion:
A Christian's life is not an easy one. We must endure hardness and fight if we would reign.

A Christian's life is a blessed one for even in the war there is a rest in Him.

- R.A. Griffin

The Dangers of Differentness

REVELATION 2:1-7

Introduction:
   One of the things on which most Christians pride themselves is their differentness from the world around them. There is a point, however, at which differentness can become a danger.

I. Commendable Differentness:
   A. They had done many good things in the Ephesian church.
   B. Among those good acts: strenuous toil, unremitting commitment, rejection of evil, trial of false prophets, steadfast endurance, quiet waiting, diligent labor and unfainting continuance.

II. Corrosive Dangers:
   A. They had confused:
      1. Eccentricity with differentness.
      2. Differentness with spirituality.
   B. They were proud and thus judgmental.
   C. They had fallen into a complacent traditionalism.

III. Challenging Diagnosis: "Thou Hast Left Thy First Love. . . "
   A. It was a "first" love both as to chronology and priorities.
   B. It was "love."
      1. For God and the Word of God.
      2. For other children of God. (One of the first signs of failure of our love for God is our failure to love the children of God.)
   C. They had "left."
      1. They had lost the fervency, depth and meaning. (Matter of the heart rather than the head.)
      2. This had happened in the process of trying the false.
      3. It had happened as they grew accustomed to things and failed to cultivate that love.
   D. The results were:
      1. Activity without reality.
      2. Orthodoxy without compassion.

IV. Correcting Directions:

A. Remember - go back to the point of departure and recognize that something has gone wrong.
B. Repent - admit that there is fault and that the fault is one's own.
C. Do - repentance is always designed to drive to action.

V. **Chastening Declaration**
A. Or else - the alternative proposed adds greater urgency.
B. Removed lampstand — church would be set aside through special judgment.
C. Means of correction — through repentance and no other way.

Conclusion:
It is possible to be different and throughly separated and still utterly fail to please God. Let us not forget our first love.

The Case of the Tolerant Church

REVELATION 2:18-29

Introduction:

The Greeks had a word for it — *hupokritos* — and it has come over into English with a similar sound — hypocrisy — and the same meaning — play acting, putting on a show.

There is much hypocrisy all around us in the modern world today and illustrations of it are plentiful in the pages of our newspapers and magazines. The church in Thyatira also had its problems with hypocrisy.

I. Note the Condition of the Church

A. Much to be commended here.
   1. Love.
   2. Service.
   3. Faith.
   4. Patience - steadfast endurance.

B. Some unusual evidence of good - " . . . the last to be more than the first . . . "
   1. This was a growing church.
   2. Some of the people were growing in these spiritual characteristics.

C. Some evidences of serious problems.
   1. There was a woman teacher (Jezebel) who was teaching others error.
   2. Not everyone in the church was involved in this, but it was being tolerated.
   3. This was such a problem, God Himself was going to deal with it.

II. Notice the Principles Involved

A. The fact that a church is growing does not necessarily mean that all is well within, because churches grow in spite of some serious internal problems.

B. The problems of churches are the problems of individuals - we like to hide behind generalities, but "the church" is people.

C. The church is held responsible for its problem people - it is the responsibility of the church to police its own affairs on the basis of Biblical discipline.

III. Notice the Personal Applications
A. What you are and what you appear to be may be two different things. Most of us have a facade, but God is not taken by appearances.
B. The individual is important in the church. You personally may be responsible for the church's failure to accomplish what God has for it to do.
C. The individual is responsible for dealing with his problems. We must not put the pressure on the church or wait for the Lord to deal very severely.

Conclusion:
Are you a hypocrite - with a good facade hiding problems which in turn cause the church problems? The need is to deal with the matter now.

A God of New Beginnings
REVELATION 21:5

Introduction:
One of the main stresses of Biblical Christianity is that of newness - the opportunity for renewal. It has been said that there are no stains or blots on the future. Each person present, no matter what the past has held, is faced with the opportunity for a new beginning in life this very day.

I. The Truth Taught
The Bible teaches that God is a God of new beginnings:
- A. He makes a *new covenant* (Jeremiah 31:31-34; Hebrews 8:7-13).
- B. He makes a *new creation* (II Corinthians 5:17).
- C. He makes a *new creature* arise out of the new creation (Ephesians 4:24; Colossians 3:10; Galatians 6:15; Ephesians 2:16).
- D. He provides a *new course* (Hebrews 10:20).
- E. He promises a *new cosmos* (Revelation 21:1).

II. The Truth Illustrated
- A. Abraham: (Genesis 11:31-12:5)
  Had come out of Ur only to settle down in Haran. God gave him a new beginning after settling into a period of dull routine.
- B. Jacob: (Genesis 25:29-33; 27:1-5; 8&9; 11&12; 15-17; 18-29)
  An opportunist and a liar, Jacob was brought to a moment of truth by his encounter with his brother, Esau. God gave a man who was too crafty, a new beginning in life.
- C. Joseph: (Genesis 37-41)
  After being victimized by a sequence of almost overwhelming circumstances, God gave Him a new beginning.
- D. Moses: (Exodus 2:11-15)
  Although properly trained and aware of his destiny, Moses failed miserably because of haste. A new beginning was given to a total failure.
- E. David: (II Samuel 11; 12:7-9; 13 & 14)
  David was guilty of lust, adultery, deceit and murder. There was a large price to pay for what had happened, but God gave a new beginning to a man who had sinned grievously.

F. Zacchaeus: (Luke 19:2-10)
    Here was a greatly hated tax-collector whom most
    everyone despised. God gave a new beginning to a
    man who was deeply unpopular.
G. Peter: (John 18:15-27)
    Peter was weak, ineffective, vacillating, etc. God gave
    a new beginning (and in the process, a great steadfast-
    ness) to a man who had been weak.
H. Paul: (Acts 8:1-3)
    Saul was opposed to God and was seeking to do all
    within his power to harm and hinder the work of the
    Lord. The Lord touched him, made him Paul and
    gave this hating, opposing blasphemer a new
    beginning.

III. The Truth Applied
A. God offers forgiveness.
    1. The simple condition is that of confession —
        agreeing with God about our sin.
    2. This forgiveness is full and complete and involves
        forgetting.
B. God promises assistance.
    1. He directly intervenes by the Holy Spirit when we
        ask Him to.
    2. He never calls us to do what we can't do.
C. God indicates success.
    1. All the men used as illustrations succeeded with
        their new start.
    2. God promised the same to us if we will trust Him.

Conclusion:
    God will take the sponge of His grace and wipe it across
the slate of the past if we will only allow Him to do so.

Believers Out of Fellowship

Introduction:
The church and the Bible are both filled with believers out of fellowship. Here are three kinds of Biblical and practical backsliders:

I. Disobedient Believers - Illustrated by Abraham in Egypt
   A. When the famine came, Abraham went into Egypt. The coming of a famine is no sign that we are in the wrong place.
   B. It is better to suffer in the place that God puts us in than to take matters into our own hands and get into endless complications.

II. Deluded Believers - Illustrated by Lot in Sodom
   A. A man seeking material things got spiritual "blight."
      1. He pitched his tent toward Sodom.
      2. He dwelt in Sodom.
      3. He sat in the gate as a leader in Sodom.
   B. To be less than out and out is to be down and out. Lot's testimony was gone and he was mocked.

III. Disgruntled Believers - Illustrated by Peter at the fire
   A. Peter's feelings were hurt when Christ rebuked him in the garden. Now he is following the enemy crowd.
   B. But Peter was upheld by Christ's prayer and we later see him at another, and much different, fire.

Conclusion:
Are you out of place? Get back to the point where you got off the track.

- Selected

The Law of Obedience

Introduction:

The whole of the Christian life is summed up in the word "obey." If we read through the book of Deuteronomy alone, we see how the Spirit of God emphasizes the importance and influence of obedience.

I. Obedience is the Proof of Repentance:

" . . . If thou turn to the Lord thy God, and shalt be obedient unto His voice," (4:30). The evidence of having turned to the Lord is response to Him in obedience.

II. Obedience is the Procurer of Blessing:

"A blessing if ye obey the commandments of the Lord your God," (11:27). We command the Lord's blessing when we respond to the Lord's word.

III. Obedience is the Preventer of Contamination:

" . . . obey His voice . . . so shalt thou put the evil away," (13:4 & 5). Obedience is the circle which encloses us and separates from the evil around.

IV. Obedience is the Evidence of Relationship:

" . . . Thou art become the people of the Lord thy God, thou shalt therefore obey the voice of the Lord thy God," (27:9&10). Because the Lord is our God, we are obligated to do His will.

V. Obedience is the Secret of Victory:

"Obey His voice . . . then the Lord thy God will return thy captivity," (30:2 & 3). Obedience is the hand that knocks off the fetters of bondage and is the cause of freedom in the Lord's service.

VI. Obedience is the Soul of Prosperity:

"Obey His voice, and the Lord thy God will make thee plenteous," (30:2, 9).

VII. Obedience is the Means of Longevity:

"Obey His voice . . . for He is thy life and the length of thy days." (30:20) Length of days and loyalty to the Lord are bound together in cause and effect.

- F.E. Marsh